ZEN GARDEN

Project Book

Learn how to create a
collection of zen gardens

5 projects inside

INTRODUCTION

Welcome to the wonderful world of Zen Gardens!

This kit has been specifically designed for adults only.

Learning a new skill is always exciting – we're here to help you get started. A Zen garden, or Japanese rock garden, is used for relaxation as well as meditation. Its purpose is to relieve stress, enhance creativity, and lower anxiety. Being small in size, you can place your own Zen garden wherever you desire - in your home or office. With so many options to choose from, you can really create a Zen garden that is completely unique to you!
Let's get your creativity flowing and open your mind to this new and unlimited world.
This kit provides everything you need to make your very own Mindfulness Zen Garden. There are also four other options, each with a step-by-step guide for you to try.
Remember, every skill takes effort to master, so don't be disheartened if it's not perfect the first time. The most important thing is that you have fun and enjoy yourself.

Let's start your Zen Garden journey!

KIT CONTENTS

WHAT'S INCLUDED:

- A Container
- 2 x Mini Faux Succulents
- A Mini Rake
- 3 x Pebbles
- Sand

YOU'LL NEED:

- A Container
- Sand
- 2 x Mini Faux Succulents
- 3 x Pebbles
- A Mini Rake

HOW DO YOU SET UP A ZEN GARDEN?

CONTAINER STYLE

You can use any container you prefer; size and shape really do not matter. Keep in mind where you might want to place it. This will help you decide how large or small your container needs to be. Do make sure that whichever size you choose, there is enough depth for the sand to fit in.

SAND

While you can choose any colour of sand, a light colour is recommended because it is the most relaxing. Of course, your garden is all about creativity, so feel free to add colours if you so desire. It is important, however, that whatever sand you choose it must be fine. This will ensure perfect patterns.

PLANTS

Again, this is your garden, so let your creativity run free when choosing plants. Being such a large part of nature, plants have a relaxing effect and compliment your garden wonderfully. There are no rules – choose from mini-trees, succulents, moss etc.

STONES

You can really let your imagination run wild with the choices of stones in your Zen garden. From beautiful patterns, to eye-catching pebbles, to balancing stones – there is no limit. Play about with some different options and see what looks and feels the best for you.

MINI ZEN GARDEN RAKE

Grab yourself a good quality rake. Uneven spikes will not produce the relaxing patterns you desire, so choose wisely with this tool.

OPTIONAL: DECORATIVE STATUES

Once again, let your imagination lead you in choosing accessories for your garden. Statues are not a must, but they can showcase your personality if you so desire. Remember, your garden is to reduce stress and anxiety and bring you peace. Choose something that will bring you joy when you look at it.

ESSENTIAL OILS

Essential oils can not only relax you, but have great healing properties too. Depending on whether you desire to feel relaxed or invigorated, there is an essential oil that will do the job. Essential oils are quite concentrated and, unlike certain synthetic fragrances, have a strong scent. Use them sparingly when dropping the oils into the sand.

THE MEANINGS BEHIND YOUR MINI ZEN GARDEN:

Zen Buddhist temples are where you would have found many Zen gardens in years gone by. Created to imitate the soft and peaceful essence of nature, they enabled people to meditate in search of an inner peacefulness, and take time out of their busy lives to contemplate their existence and the meaning of life. Composed of gravel, sand and rocks, each element of a Zen garden has its own meaning.

SAND AND GRAVEL:

Purity, emptiness and distance. These are the qualities attributed to water, the element symbolised by gravel and sand. Because sand is easily disturbed by wind and rain, gravel is used as a heavier option.

RAKING:

The pattern created by the rake, represents the waves or ripples of water. It takes much concentration to achieve perfect lines, and with the mind in a state of focus, the practice of concentration and meditation can be implemented. Challenge yourself by developing variations in your patterns.

ROCKS AND STONES:

Rocks, stones and pebbles can have various meanings such as; mountains, islands, rivers and waterfalls.

ZEN GARDENS FOR STRESS AND ANXIETY RELIEF:

Life can get very busy very quickly, and we can often find ourselves swept away in the rush of it all. The act of raking the sand in your Zen garden and arranging the stones, brings an immediate effect of relaxation. By focusing on the present moment, we cannot overthink or stress about the past or future. Taking a few minutes every day, whether at home or in the office, to meditate on your life, will bring great benefits to your health and well-being.

ZEN GARDENS TO IMPROVE MEDITATION SKILLS:

Meditation is nothing new. People have been doing it for thousands of years. The benefits of mediation have been recorded and documented many times over. If you have never meditated before, your Zen garden will assist you in getting in the right frame of mind. Concentrating on your breathing while raking the sand is a perfect way to do this. It also quietens your thoughts. Some thoughts will arise, but acknowledge them and let them go. With practice, you will find you slip into this state of mind easier each time, until your mind will eventually quieten itself will little effort. Guided meditations are also very beneficial for improving your mediation skills.

ZEN GARDENS TO ENHANCE CREATIVITY:

By meditating, you open your mind to more creative thinking. It can assist you, not only in allowing new ideas to flow, but in areas of problem solving too.

ZEN GARDENS TO INCREASE YOUR FOCUS AND DEDICATION:

To practice meditation, you will need to focus. Therefore, the more you practice, the easier it will be to focus and dedicate your attention to the things that need it the most. It will also improve your patience and self-control.

WARNINGS!

All the makes included in this book are designed specifically for adults. Never put pebbles/stones, sand and faux plants in your mouth.

Keep all kit contents and finished products out of the reach of children.

Do not ingest; if accidentally ingested, drink water and seek medical advice.

To avoid danger of suffocation, keep plastic bags away from your head. Some ingredients may irritate; always avoid contact with skin and eyes. If ingredients come into contact with eyes or skin, wash with cold water immediately.

MINDFULNESS ZEN GARDEN

MINDFULNESS ZEN GARDEN

Become a mindful version of yourself with this mini Zen garden. Place your garden in any space in your home or office where you feel everyone can use it the most. Make this Zen garden a part of your daily mindful routine. Whether that means tracing over sand patterns or routinely creating new patterns – the choice is up to you! The use of these complementary faux plants, adds tranquility and helps inspire positive well-being, just like mini Zen gardens.

KIT INCLUDES
- Container
- Succulents
- Rake
- Pebbles
- Sand

OPTIONAL
- Decorative Statues
- Jojoba Oil

METHOD

1. Fill your container with sand. Add a few drops of essential oil into the sand if you want. Shake the container to even out the sand.
Optional Pro tip: if you want to have a wet looking sand, add a few drops of all-natural jojoba oil to make your sand patterns stand out.

2. Place plants onto the sand. Plants are a great way to bring nature into your mini Zen garden. However, plants aren't necessary elements in mini Zen gardens. If you are using real plants, add them before pouring the sand. Use your pebbles as a divider into the sand before adding the plants.

3. Adding stones and rocks onto the sand are very beautiful and important elements in desktop Zen gardens. You can add them into the corner as a group or just place them separately from each other – this is basically up to you and what you prefer. One very interesting mini Zen garden idea is to add balancing stones – it's a great eye catcher.

4. Optional: Place your favourite statues and accessories onto the sand to make a relaxing decoration. Some great ideas for statues and mini Zen garden accessories are, for example; miniature pandas or laughing Buddha statues. Choose something that makes you happy and relaxed. Why not try a miniature bonsai tree?

5. Start raking! Now you are ready to create the most enjoyable patterns. Use the regular mini Zen garden rakes or try something new like mini zen garden stamps!

Now you have your own mini Zen garden! Place it onto your desk or in a room of your choice where you can meditate and practice mindfulness anytime you want.

NOTES

Use the space below to make your own personal notes on the previous project to help when you come back to make it again!

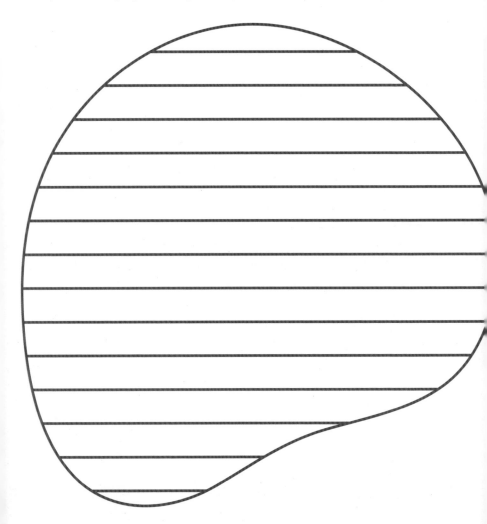

QUIRKY GARDEN

QUIRKY GARDEN

You can use your Zen garden to represent a setting that is personally peaceful to you. Choose your favourite sand colour, this seaside Zen garden is perfect for any fond beach goer!

WHAT YOU WILL NEED
· White Container
· Blue Sand
· Rake
· Shells
· Polished Stones
· Faux Plant

METHOD

1. Fill your container with the blue sand.

2. Place shells onto the sand. Shells are a great way to bring nature into your mini Zen garden. These shells will help create that relaxing atmosphere of being on the beach.

3. Add in your fun beach-themed trinkets to add to the beach ambience.

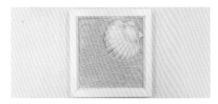

4. Start raking! Now you are ready to create the most enjoyable patterns. Use the regular mini zen garden rakes.

5. Scatter polished stones around your garden to match the light colour scheme.

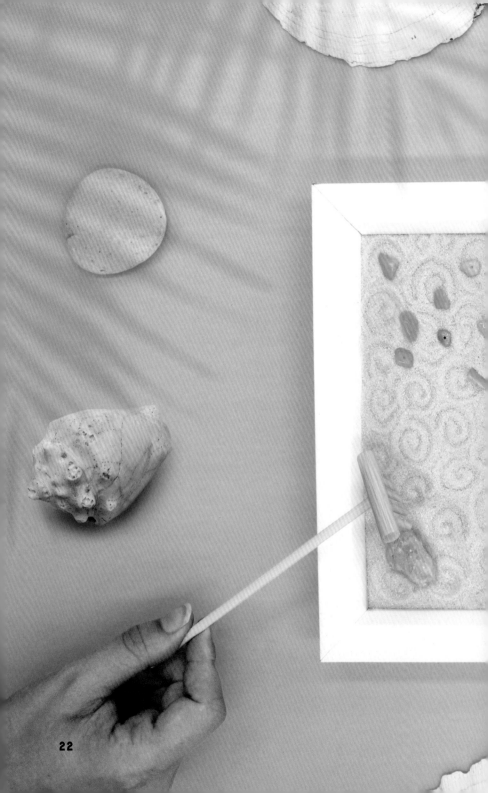

NOTES

Use the space below to make your own personal notes on the previous project to help when you come back to make it again!

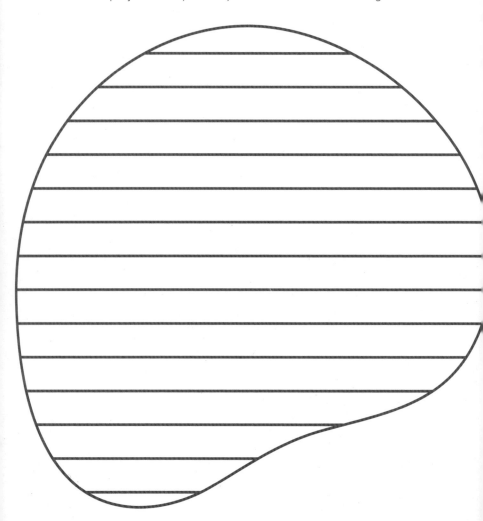

MODERN GARDEN

MODERN GARDEN

Support your serenity, understanding, trust and grace with this modern amethyst stone-filled Zen garden!

WHAT YOU WILL NEED

· Wooden Rectangular Container
· White Sand
· Amethyst Crystals
·Faux Plant
· Rake
· Polished Stones

METHOD

1. Fill your container with the white sand.

2. Place your amethyst crystals into your mini Zen garden. These amethyst stones are a symbol of serenity, understanding, trust and grace.

3. Add in your faux plant for extra tranquillity.

4. Start raking! Now you are ready to create the most enjoyable patterns. Use the regular mini zen garden rakes.

5. Scatter polished stones around your garden to match the light colour scheme.

NOTES

Use the space below to make your own personal notes on the previous project to help when you come back to make it again!

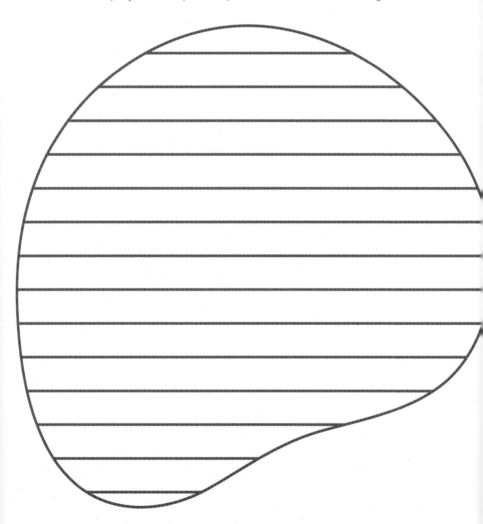

JADE GARDEN

JADE GARDEN

Unwind with this jade-themed Zen garden. Jade crystals are a symbol of serenity and purity, perfect for relaxing in the evenings!

WHAT YOU WILL NEED

· Tealight Candle
· Jade Crystals
· Rake
· Polished Stones
· Pagoda Statue
· White Sand
· Black Divided Container

METHOD

1. Fill your container with the white sand.

2. Place your jade crystals and polished stones into your mini Zen garden. These jade stones are a symbol of serenity and purity.

3. Add your pagoda statue to your Zen garden. Pagoda's are a place of contemplation, spiritual tranquillity - a bridge between the natural world and the spiritual world.

4. Start raking! Now you are ready to create the most enjoyable patterns. Use the regular mini zen garden rakes.

5. Add your candle to your last container section. Light your candle to complete your calming zen garden.

NOTES

Use the space below to make your own personal notes on the previous project to help when you come back to make it again!

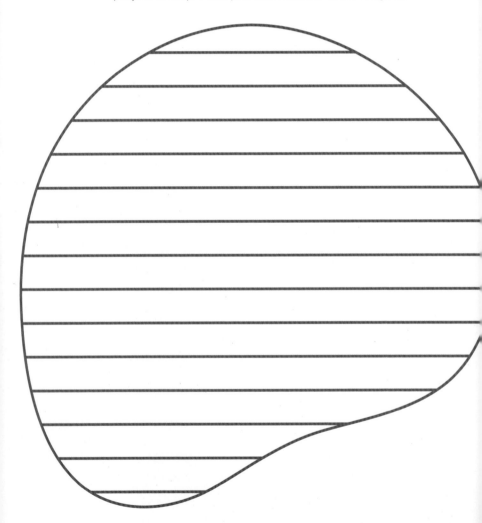

MINIMALIST
ZEN GARDEN

MINIMALIST ZEN GARDEN

Create a happier mindset with this minimalist Zen garden. Minimalism has been proven to aid in lowering stress levels.

WHAT YOU WILL NEED
- Faux plants
- Rake
- Polished Stones
- Buddha Statue
- White, Beige & Black Sand
- Concrete Divided Container

METHOD

1. Pour the different colours of sand into the separate sections of your concrete container. Shake it from side to side to even it out.

2. Place your faux plants into your mini Zen garden.

3. Add your Buddha statue to your Zen garden. Buddha statues encourage the onlooker to draw from within and turn a negative into a positive.

4. Start raking! Now you are ready to create the most enjoyable patterns. Use the regular mini Zen garden rakes.

5. Scatter polished stones around your garden to match the minimalist colour scheme.

45

NOTES

Use the space below to make your own personal notes on the previous project to help when you come back to make it again!

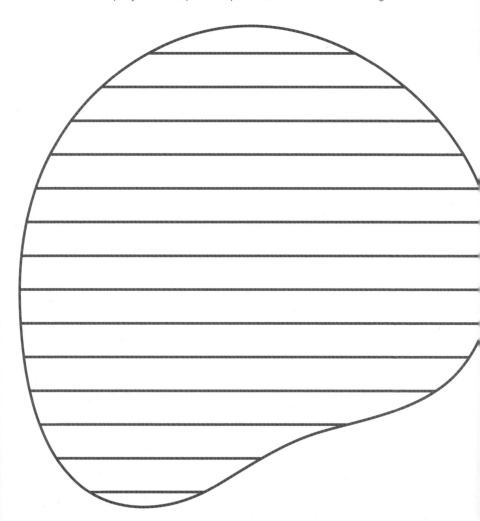